MAKING
HEALTHY
FOOD
CHOICES

Do You Know Where Your Food Comes From

Neil Morris

www.heinemann.co.uk/library

Visit our website to find out more information about Heinemann Library books.

To order:

 Phone 44 (0) 1865 888066

 Send a fax to 44 (0) 1865 314091

 Visit the Heinemann Bookshop at www.heinemann.co.uk/library to browse our catalogue and order online.

First published in Great Britain by Heinemann Library, Halley Court, Jordan Hill, Oxford OX2 8EJ, part of Harcourt Education.
Heinemann is a registered trademark of Harcourt Education Ltd.

Editorial: Andrew Farrow and
    Christine McCafferty
Design: David Poole and Geoff Ward
Picture Research: Melissa Allison and
    Maria Joannou
Production: Chloe Bloom

Originated by Chroma
Printed and bound in China by South China Printing Company

10 digit ISBN 0 431 11917 1
13 digit ISBN 978 0 431 11917 5
10 09 08 07 06
10 9 8 7 6 5 4 3 2 1

British Library Cataloguing in Publication Data
Morris, Neil, 1946-
Where does your food come from?. -
(Making healthy food choices)
363.8
A full catalogue record for this book is available from the British Library.

Acknowledgements
The publishers would like to thank the following for permission to reproduce photographs:

Alamy Images p. 25 (Robert Harding); Corbis pp. 4, 6 (Gail Mooney), 7 (Wolfgang Kaehler), 9, 11 (Henry Romero/Reuters), 18 (Bohemian Nomad Picturemakers), Corbis 21 top, 22 (David Samuel Robbins), 23 (Pablo Corral V), 28 (David Muench), 29 (Jeremy Horner), 30 (James L. Amos), 31 (Michelle Garrett), 33 top, 34 (Giry Daniel), 35 (Vittoriano Rastelli), 41 (Amanda Gazidis; Ecoscene), 45 (Mark Peterson), 47 (Carl & Ann Purcell); Getty Images pp. 12 (Stone/ Gary John Norman), 13 (Stone/ Peter Cade), 19 (Paul S. Howell/ Liaison), 27 (Stone), 33 bott (Taxi/ Allan H Shoemake), 38 (Lambert), 43 (Robert Harding), 46 (Lonely Planet/ Angus Oborn), 49 (Image Bank/ Lambert); Harcourt Education Ltd pp. 50 and 51 (MM Studios),; Lonely Planet Images p. 24 (Lindsay Brown); Maria Joannou p. 40; Photolibrary p. 21 bott (Foodpix/ Joe Pellegrini); Rex Features pp. 14 (Garo / Phanie), 37, 42 (JIAN CHEN). Symbols on p. 10 www.transfairusa.org and www.fairtrade.org.uk

Cover photograph of rows of eggs reproduced with permission of Getty Images (Image Bank/ Stephen Marks).

The publishers would like to thank Rebecca Weeden for her assistance in the preparation of this book.

CONTENTS

Any words appearing in the text in bold, **like this**,
are explained in the glossary.

THE WORLD OF FOOD !
– we can't live without it

Food is one of our most important basic needs. However, do you ever wonder where your food comes from? Many of the ingredients were probably bought in your local supermarket. But where were the vegetables grown originally, and what kind of farm produced the meat? Is it local food, or has it travelled halfway across the world?

We cannot do without food. It provides us with the energy we need for everything we do. There are all sorts of foods grown in different parts of the world. This means we have a wide selection to choose from. The choices we make are important for our health, and where our food comes from might affect some of those choices.

WORLD TRADE NETWORK

In developing countries around the world, many families farm the land and grow their own food. Others buy food from local farmers. But in the richer, more developed countries, most people depend on the food industry. They buy their food from shops and supermarkets. This is made possible by a **world trade network** in food.

▶ People of all ages can enjoy eating a family meal together. Food is a basic need – but it can also be fun.

Many countries produce more food than they need, but others do not produce enough. Those with a **surplus export** it to other countries. Exporting and **importing** countries form a world network.

In many parts of the world, **crop** farming is big business. Big companies trade the staple foods that form the basis of people's diet. These include the leading crops of wheat, rice, **sorghum**, and maize. The table below shows where the major **cereal grains** are produced, and which countries export and import the most. You will see that the top producers are not always the biggest exporters. The figures depend on how much food countries need for their own people.

Cereal grains: the world's top five producers and trading countries

grain in millions of metric tonnes (US tons) per year		1st	2nd	3rd	4th	5th
barley	produced	Russia 18.0 (19.8)	Canada 13.0 (14.3)	Germany 13.0 (14.3)	Ukraine 11.1 (12.2)	France 11.0 (12.1)
	exported	France 5.5 (6.8)	Germany 3.2 (3.5)	Russia 3.1 (3.4)	Ukraine 1.9 (2.1)	UK 1.1 (1.2)
	imported	Japan 1.4 (1.5)	China 1.4 (0.5)	Belgium 1.2 (1.3)	Netherlands 1.2 (1.3)	Italy 0.9 (1.0)
maize	produced	USA 298.0 (328.4)	China 131.7 (145.1)	Brazil 42.0 (46.3)	Mexico 20.0 (22)	France 15.7 (17.3)
	exported	USA 43.0 (47.4)	China 16.4 (18.1)	Argentina 11.9 (13.1)	France 7.1 (7.8)	Hungary 1.3 (1.4)
	imported	Japan 17.0 (18.7)	South Korea 8.8 (9.7)	Mexico 5.8 (6.4)	Taiwan 5.1 (5.6)	Egypt 4.1 (4.5)
rice	produced	China 185.1 (203.9)	India 124.4 (137.1)	Indonesia 53.1 (58.5)	Bangladesh 37.9 (41.8)	Vietnam 35.5 (39.1)
	exported	USA 2.0 (2.2)	Uruguay 0.1 (0.1)	Argentina 0.04 (0.04)	India 0.03 (0.03)	France 0.02 (0.02)
	imported	Mexico 0.7 (0.8)	Brazil 0.7 (0.8)	Turkey 0.2 (0.2)	Costa Rica 0.2 (0.2)	Nicaragua 0.1 (0.1)
sorghum	produced	USA 11.7 (12.9)	Nigeria 8.1 (8.9)	India 6.5 (7.2)	Mexico 6.3 (6.9)	Sudan 5.2 (5.7)
	exported	USA 5.0 (5.5)	Argentina 0.7 (0.8)	France 0.2 (0.2)	China 0.1 (0.1)	Brazil 0.03 (0.03)
	imported	Mexico 3.4 (3.7)	Japan 1.5 (1.7)	Spain 0.7 (0.8)	Italy 0.3 (0.3)	Israel 0.1 (0.1)
wheat	produced	China 91.3 (100.6)	India 72.1 (79.5)	USA 58.9 (64.9)	Russia 42.2 (46.5)	France 39.6 (43.6)
	exported	USA 25.1 (27.7)	France 16.4 (18.1)	Canada 11.7 (12.9)	Australia 9.5 (10.5)	Russia 7.6 (8.4)
	imported	Italy 7.0 (7.7)	Brazil 6.6 (7.3)	Japan 5.2 (5.7)	Egypt 4.1 (4.5)	Spain 3.9 (4.3)

INTERNATIONAL CITIES

Do you live in a town or city? Approximately half of the world's population do, and the numbers are increasing all the time. In richer countries, three out of every four people live in urban areas. It will be four in every five by 2030. As well as moving from the countryside to the town, people are also moving from country to country.

The result is that modern cities have a variety of people. In many cities people with similar backgrounds form their own communities. Many large cities in Europe and North America have their own Chinatown, for example. Multicultural cities offer a wide range of foodstuffs, so that individual communities can have a choice of their own traditional meals.

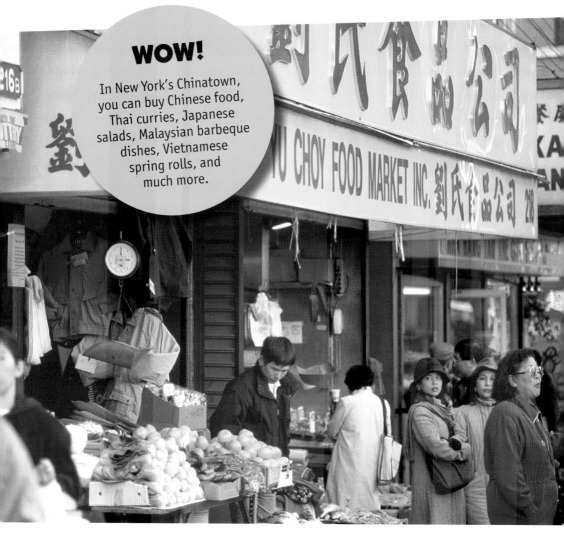

WOW!

In New York's Chinatown, you can buy Chinese food, Thai curries, Japanese salads, Malaysian barbeque dishes, Vietnamese spring rolls, and much more.

▲ There are plenty of busy food shops and restaurants in New York's Chinatown district.

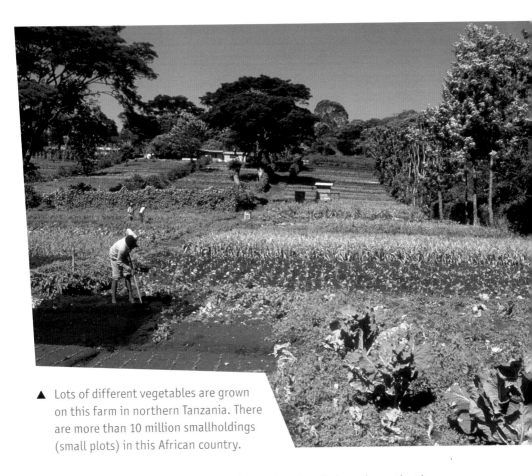

▲ Lots of different vegetables are grown on this farm in northern Tanzania. There are more than 10 million smallholdings (small plots) in this African country.

The food industry is geared towards making food cheaply so that it is affordable to buy. Many people think that healthy food is still too expensive, but is it really? If people in the developed world were prepared to pay more for their food, it would help farmers and food producers everywhere. Rich countries might also be able to afford to give more food aid to developing countries. What do you think – should developed countries pay more for their food?

Food for all?

- ✔ Enough food is produced all over the world for every person in the world to take in more than 2,700 calories of energy every day. This is more than enough for good health. However, many people do not have enough land to grow the food they need or enough money to buy food.

- ✔ At least 800 million people (12 per cent of the world's population) do not have enough food to lead healthy lives. They are starving.

COMMERCIAL AGRICULTURE
– the world's most important industry

In the developing world, most farmers produce just enough food for themselves and their families. They are called subsistence farmers. Those who manage to produce more food than they need sell the excess as cash crops.

Many subsistence farmers, especially in Africa, use the same methods as their ancestors did hundreds of years ago. They do all the work themselves and have very little machinery. But commercial farmers, and especially those in richer countries, have found new ways to increase food production. Commercial agriculture is the world's most important industry because it provides us with all our food. Modern methods involve using more and bigger machines, which are expensive. This means that large-scale farms need a lot of money to start and run.

Mechanized farms employ fewer people. Yet about half the world's workers are still employed in agriculture. This is more than in any other industry.

MIXED FARMS

Many commercial farms grow a range of crops, and many raise a variety of animals. This is called mixed farming. Most European farms are mixed farms. They have the advantage that they can sell a range of food to local markets and shops. If there is a problem with one of their crops, because of bad weather or disease for example, it is not disastrous for farmers. They can still make money from other crops and animals.

In industrialized countries, many farms have become bigger but more specialized. This is especially the case in the United States, where the vast majority of farms are specialized and often take up huge areas of land. Potato and dairy farms are good examples of specialized agriculture. About 300 million tonnes of potatoes are produced around the world every year, and a quarter of them are grown in China. In 2005 scientists traced the history of the first ever potato back to Peru more than 7,000 years ago. All modern varieties are descended from this, but today Peru produces far fewer potatoes than the United Kingdom or the United States.

On specialized dairy farms, large herds of cows are kept for their milk. Dairy farming techniques have changed dramatically over the years. Cows used to be milked by hand, which took a long time and needed many farmhands. Today, farmers use milking machines. This makes it more profitable for the farmer and cheaper for the consumer.

Potatoes and milk: the world's top five producers and importers

millions of metric tonnes (US tons)		1st	2nd	3rd	4th	5th
potatoes	produced	China 75.0 (82.7)	Russia 37.0 (40.8)	India 25.0 (27.6)	USA 20.4 (22.5)	Ukraine 19.5 (21.5)
	imported	Netherlands 1.8 (2.0)	Belgium 1.0 (1.1)	Spain 0.7 (0.8)	Italy 0.6 (0.7)	Germany 0.6 (0.7)
cows' milk	produced	USA 77.6 (85.5)	India 37.8 (41.7)	Russia 30.9 (34.1)	Germany 28.0 (30.9)	France 24.2 (26.0)
	imported	Italy 1.4 (1.5)	Germany 1.2 (1.3)	Belgium 0.8 (0.9)	France 0.4 (0.4)	Spain 0.3 (0.3)

▲ Farmers in Wisconsin, USA, plough their fields according to the contours of the land. There are many dairy, cereal, and vegetable farms in the state.

HELPING SMALL FARMERS

Like many other people, you would probably like to help farmers in poorer parts of the world. What if you were able to choose food items produced by small farmers rather than by giant food companies? Well, now you can, by looking for a Fairtrade label on the food you buy.

Millions of small farmers in the developing world find it difficult to make a proper living. They often have to sell their produce to big companies rather than directly to customers. When prices are low, they earn very little. The Fairtrade system means that they can earn a fair amount for good produce.

The Fairtrade label first appeared in Europe in 1986, when a Dutch company bought coffee directly from small suppliers in Mexico. The idea spread quickly, and now 21 countries are members of an organization called Fairtrade International.

When you see this symbol on a product, it means that it has been checked by Fairtrade International. The mark on the top left is used in the United States. The mark at the bottom right is used in the United Kingdom, most of Europe, and Japan.

The farmers who produced the original crop were paid a fair price. You may find the logo on bananas and other fresh fruit, or juices, honey, coffee, tea, chocolate, cocoa, sugar, nuts, and sometimes even on flowers.

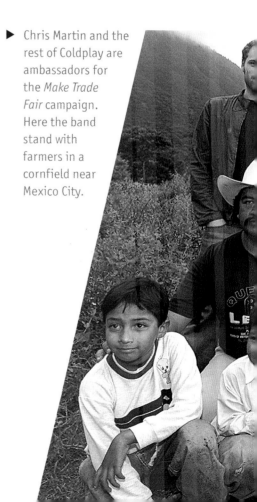

▶ Chris Martin and the rest of Coldplay are ambassadors for the *Make Trade Fair* campaign. Here the band stand with farmers in a cornfield near Mexico City.

FRAGRANT HIMALAYAN RICE

India is the world's second largest producer of rice. In the northern Indian state of Uttaranchal, in the foothills of the Himalayan Mountains, small farmers specialize in growing long-grain rice. They call their rice basmati, which in the Hindi language means "fragrant", because it has a lovely nutty smell. In the past, the Himalayan farmers sold their rice to **agents** at the local market and often received very low prices. This made it hard for them to support their families.

In 2003, a group of more than 500 growers joined the Fairtrade scheme. Now they receive a guaranteed price for their high-quality rice. This has made it possible for them to help other villagers build new roads and improve local schools.

Many supermarkets have introduced own-label Fairtrade foods (that is, with the supermarket's name on). In 2005, the United Kingdom's largest supermarket chain started selling Fairtrade Himalayan basmati rice. It is also sold in the United States.

INTENSIVE FARMING

Some farmers use special methods to produce the greatest amount of crops, meat, or eggs in the shortest time and for the smallest cost. This is known as **intensive farming**. The advantage is that the cost savings can be passed on to the consumer. This makes food cheaper which many people say is a good thing, especially for poorer people.

However, there are problems with intensive farming. One problem is that the quality of produce can drop along with the costs, especially where animals are concerned. Animals kept in conditions where they cannot move about freely are less healthy than those that lead freer lives. This usually means that the quality of their meat, milk, or eggs is not as good. Many people also think that intensive methods are cruel because animals need space, sunlight, and fresh air to lead healthy lives.

BATTERY, BARN, OR FREE-RANGE EGGS?

To produce the most and cheapest eggs, **battery hens** are kept in indoor cages. Their eggs roll down from the cage and are caught in a trough.

WOW!

It is estimated that there are 4.7 billion egg-laying hens in the world. About 75 per cent are kept in cages, but more will probably be kept indoors in the future.

▲ Rows of chickens in a battery farm. Many people think that battery farming is cruel and should be banned.

Barn eggs are produced by hens that are kept in loose flocks inside sheds (or "barns"). The birds are allowed to roam throughout the barn. Free-range hens lead more natural lives. They wander about the farm during the day, and at night go into purpose-built hen houses.

A recent study showed that free-range eggs have more **vitamin** A and higher levels of **omega-3** fatty acids, which are very good for human health. The **nutrients** in eggs are also dependent on the quality of feed given to hens. You therefore have a choice of eggs. Those from a battery may be labelled "eggs from caged hens". If the label does not say where the eggs came from, you can assume it was a battery farm. Barn and free-range eggs will certainly be labelled, and are more expensive.

BIRD FLU PROBLEMS

IIn 2005–2006 there was a scare that migrating birds were carrying a disease called avian flu (also called bird flu) around the world. The wild birds could infect free-range hens and other farm birds, so experts advised keeping poultry indoors. This meant an increase in barn hens. Although there was no evidence that the deadly H5N1 bird-flu virus could be passed to humans by eating infected poultry, some countries began destroying farm birds and vaccinating others. Bird flu is bound to have a big effect on the free-range farming of poultry.

▼ These English pigs are allowed to roam. Their meat will be sold as "outdoor-reared pork".

FISHING

Fish is a major foodstuff. Years ago fishing fleets were made up of small boats. People who lived near the coast waited for the day's catch and had a choice of fish at the market. This is still how things work in small fishing villages all over the world. Choice is limited by what happens to be caught that day.

Things are very different in other countries though. Large fishing fleets are made up of huge **factory ships**. These vessels can travel across the world's oceans, make big catches, and even freeze the fish on board. Most of the fish in your supermarket will have been caught this way, especially the fish sold in the frozen section.

▼ These fishermen are sorting and packing their large catch of sardines.

People fish all over the world, in rivers as well as the oceans. You will find frozen fish in your supermarket, as well as canned fish such as tuna and sardines.

Some fish is also **cured** (smoked, dried, or salted). Just over half the fish caught is sold fresh, more than a quarter is frozen, and the rest is canned or cured.

Fish farming, or aquaculture, is also practised all over the world. Fish such as salmon are reared in freshwater tanks and then kept in large sea water pens near the coast. Experts say that this is the fastest growing sector of animal food production. The biggest fish-farming nations are in south and east Asia. They are China, India, Indonesia, Vietnam, and Japan.

PROTEIN AND FAT

All kinds of fish contain a lot of **protein**, which is an important nutrient. High-protein meat, eggs, and fish should make up about 10–15 per cent of our diet.

Fish are quite low in fat, but oily fish such as mackerel, herring, and sardines contain lots of the healthy kind of fat called omega-3. They are also a very good source of vitamins A and D.

Many people believe that omega-3 fatty acids can benefit the heart and circulation of people, and that it especially helps those who have had heart attacks and heart disease. Some people claim that it can also beat depression. Some research has even shown that these fatty acids can make you more intelligent. Some manufacturers advertise their fish oil as "brain food"! Whether this is true or not, we should be eating at least two portions of fish a week, including one portion of oily, omega-3-rich fish.

Comparing oily fish		
100 g portion	**protein in grams**	**omega-3 fatty acids in grams**
anchovy	20.4	1.4
herring	24.5	1.8
mackerel	25.4	2.2
sardine	20.0	1.7
tuna	25.0	1.6

Labels will tell you whether fish is farmed or caught. If the fish was caught, it will tell you where. China catches by far the most fish, and is also the largest exporter. Japan imports the most.

The two fish most often caught are anchovy and pollock, and both live in Pacific waters. The blue whiting lives in the eastern Atlantic, and tuna can cross oceans or even move from one ocean to another.

The world's biggest fishers

total catch in millions of metric tonnes (US tons) per year		exports in millions of US $		imports in millions of US $	
China	16.8 (18.5)	China	5.2	Japan	12.4
Peru	6.1 (6.7)	Thailand	0.9	USA	11.7
USA	4.9 (5.4)	Norway	3.6	Spain	4.9
Indonesia	4.7 (5.2)	USA	3.4	France	3.8
Japan	4.6 (5.1)	Canada	3.3	Italy	3.6
India	3.7 (4.1)	Denmark	3.2	Germany	2.6
Chile	3.6 (4.0)	Spain	2.2	UK	2.5
Russia	3.3 (3.6)	Vietnam	2.2	China	2.4
Thailand	2.8 (3.1)	Netherlands	2.2	Denmark	2.1
Norway	2.6 (2.9)	Chile	2.1	South Korea	1.9

OVERFISHING

In many regions there are simply too many fishermen catching too many fish. This means that fish populations are in decline. The Atlantic cod, for example, used to be one of the most popular fish to eat in Europe and the United States. But it has been so heavily overfished that less than half as much is sold today as in 1988. Stocks in some areas, including the North Sea, are so low that some experts believe that cod fishing should be banned altogether. The populations of hake, haddock, and flounder have also fallen dramatically.

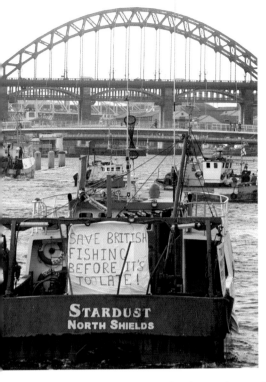

The most frequently caught fish species	
in millions of metric tonnes (US tons) per year	
Peruvian anchovy	6.2 (6.8)
Alaska pollock	2.9 (3.2)
blue whiting	2.4 (2.6)
skipjack tuna	2.1 (2.3)
Japanese anchovy	2.1 (2.3)
Atlantic herring	2.0 (2.2)
chub mackerel	1.9 (2.1)
Chilean jack mackerel	1.7 (1.9)
yellowfin tuna	1.5 (1.7)
largehead hairtail	1.5 (1.7)

▲ Fishermen protesting in north-east England about European quotas. These limit the amount of fish they are allowed to catch in the North Sea. The quotas are set by the European Union for all its member states.

EXPERTS RECOMMEND COD CATCH BAN

"Scientists have recommended that cod fishing is banned in the seas around Scotland. Experts working for the International Council for the Exploration of the Sea (ICES) said it was the only way that **depleted** cod stocks could recover. [...] They also want to see cuts in catches of North Sea plaice and sole, and restrictions on catching effort for monkfish."

From BBC News at bbcnews.com © bbc.co.uk, October 2005

Modern fishing methods are so effective that there is often a large by-catch. Unwanted fish are caught in the same nets as the fish that are wanted. Some of this by-catch includes species that are **endangered**. Whales, dolphins, seals, and turtles are often killed as by-catch. According to the environmental group Greenpeace, 100 million sharks are killed each year. They say that tuna fisheries alone catch more than a million sharks. An estimated 300,000 whales and dolphins die each year, because they cannot escape when caught accidentally in tuna nets.

CHOOSING ORGANIC

Many people care a great deal about what kind of farm their food comes from. They prefer their food to be produced without the use of **pesticides** or artificial **fertilizers**.

Food items labelled "organic" must come from land that has been farmed naturally for at least two years. However, if food products have only some organic ingredients then the food label must reflect that. **Manure** is widely used as an organic fertilizer. It is constantly available on farms that have livestock. Another approach is to rotate crops from year to year, alternating with plants such as alfalfa. This **leguminous** plant restores **nitrogen** to the soil to make it more fertile.

▲ These rows of raspberry bushes grow on an organic farm near the Cascade Mountains of north-west United States.

Agritourism

✔ Agritourism (short for agricultural tourism) helps keep some small farms in business. It is especially useful for small organic farms. Families can go and stay at a farm in California and enjoy organic avocados, or on an Australian farm where the speciality is tropical fruits.

✔ Small dairy farms are popular in the United Kingdom. Holidaymakers can enjoy watching traditional methods of farming, and can even help with some work.

FOOD WITHOUT SOIL

How would you feel about eating vegetables that have never touched soil? You probably already have, without even knowing it. The process of growing food plants in sand, gravel or sawdust is called hydroponics. It is used more and more, but is rarely mentioned on food labels. Nutrient solutions and water help the plants grow, usually under the protection of a plastic greenhouse.

The system is very successful but costs a lot. It is good for growing high-quality tomatoes, cucumbers, salad crops, and herbs. There is a large growing area near the coast of southern Spain. There are huge areas of plastic-covered "fields" (without any soil), where the farmers practise controlled environment agriculture (CEA).

▼ Thirty different kinds of vegetables are grown in this hydroponic greenhouse in Houston, Texas, USA. The growers are checking butterhead lettuce.

AROUND THE WORLD
– what is made where, and when

Food production depends on climate. Some plants prefer a mild climate, while others grow better where it is generally hotter or colder. The same is true of farm animals. In the past this meant that particular foods were available in certain parts of the world at certain times. Availability depended on the season.

The world trade network means that today many foods are available all year round. It allows produce to be exported during summertime from one part of the world to another region where it is winter.

WORLD OF WHEAT

Wheat is probably the world's most important food crop. It generally grows best in cool climates with moderate rainfall. China is the world's leading producer of wheat, and the United States is the largest exporter (see page 5). Wheat harvests are affected by the weather, but it is usually being harvested somewhere in the world at any time.

Most wheat is ground into flour. Much of this is used to make bread, as well as cakes, biscuits, and breakfast cereals. A special kind of wheat, called durum (meaning "hard") is used to make pasta. It is grown in dry regions.

Monthly wheat harvests around the world	
January	Chile, New Zealand
February	Chile, Myanmar, New Zealand
March	Egypt, India
April	Egypt, India, Iran, Mexico
May	China, Japan, Spain, USA
June	China, Greece, Spain, Turkey, USA
July	Bulgaria, France, Germany, Hungary, Russia, UK, Ukraine, USA
August	Canada, Denmark, Russia, UK, Ukraine, USA
September	Canada, Russia, Scandinavian countries, Scotland
October	Kazakhstan, Norway, Sweden
November	Argentina, Australia, Brazil, South Africa
December	Argentina, Australia

Wheat is used for many other foods too

✔ *bulgur* – cereal food from Turkey made from whole wheat partially boiled then dried and cracked

✔ *couscous* – North African semolina made from crushed durum wheat

✔ *freekeh* – roasted green wheat popular in Arab countries

✔ *frumenty* – old English wheat porridge with milk and spices

✔ *semolina* – hard grains left after milling wheat, used in puddings and pasta

✔ *sprouted wheat* – salad or cooked vegetable popular with vegetarians.

▶ After wheat has been harvested, the grain is loaded on to a truck. It is then taken from the farm to a granary.

▼ There are lots of different types of bread. Regional specialities have become popular all over the world.

REFINED VERSUS UNREFINED

Grains of wheat are made up of **kernels**. These contain a **husk** called bran, a soft inner part called endosperm, and an **embryo** called a germ. To make white flour (and white bread), millers remove the bran and germ and grind the endosperm only. This refined flour lacks some of the vitamins and **minerals** present in the bran and germ. Wholewheat or wholegrain flour is made from the entire kernel, and nutritionists say this is better for you.

TRAVELLING FRUIT

There are thousands of different apple varieties, but most supermarkets sell just a few. Up to 100 varieties are grown commercially in the United States. In the United Kingdom, where 30 varieties are grown, orchards find it difficult to compete with imported produce. Two-thirds of the apples eaten in the United Kingdom are grown elsewhere.

These days many apples are labelled with their name and country of origin. Take a look next time to see – you might get a surprise. The biggest apple exporters to Britain are France, South Africa, and New Zealand. The United States imports most apples from Chile, New Zealand, and Canada.

▲ Different kinds of apples are for sale at this US market, giving customers a wide choice.

Apple origins

✔ Bramley is an English cooking apple. The first Bramley tree grew from pips planted by a young girl in about 1809. The original tree still bears fruit today.

✔ Golden Delicious is now the most widely grown apple in many countries. It first appeared in West Virginia, USA, around 1900.

✔ Granny Smith is a shiny green apple that grows well in Australia, Chile, France, and South Africa. But who was Granny Smith? She was an Australian – Maria Anne Smith, of Sydney – who first grew this variety around 1865.

✔ McIntosh is a Canadian variety, discovered around 1811 by John McIntosh in Ontario. Now there are more than 3 million McIntosh trees in North America.

✔ Royal Gala was developed in New Zealand and may originally have come from a form of the English Cox's Orange Pippin.

**Fruit: the world's biggest producers
in millions of metric tonnes (US tons) per year**

apples	bananas	lemons/limes	oranges	papayas
China 20.5 (22.6)	India 16.8 (18.5)	Mexico 1.8 (2.0)	Brazil 18.3 (20.2)	Brazil 1.6 (1.8)
USA 4.3 (4.7)	Brazil 6.6 (7.3)	India 1.4 (1.5)	USA 11.7 (12.9)	Mexico 1.0 (1.1)
Poland 2.5 (2.8)	China 6.0 (6.6)	Iran 1.1 (1.2)	Mexico 4.0 (4.4)	Nigeria 0.8 (0.9)
France 2.4 (2.6)	Ecuador 5.9 (6.5)	Spain 1.1 (1.2)	India 3.1 (3.4)	India 0.7 (0.8)
Iran 2.4 (2.6)	Philippines 5.5 (6.1)	Argentina 1.0 (1.1)	Spain 2.9 (3.2)	Indonesia 0.7 (0.8)

Bananas are a very popular fruit. The two main production regions of bananas are ACP (African, Caribbean, and Pacific countries such as Cameroon and St Lucia) and Central and South America. Many Caribbean bananas are produced on small farms, usually owned by local family farmers. In Central and South America, many farms are owned by large **corporations**. They produce what are often called "dollar bananas" because many companies are US owned.

In Europe most consumers have a choice between the two regions, because bananas are labelled with their country of origin. St Lucia (a small Caribbean island) exports almost all its bananas to the United Kingdom. In the United States, which is the world's largest importer, most bananas come from Ecuador, Costa Rica, and Guatemala.

◀ Loading bananas at a port in Ecuador, South America. Ecuador is the world's largest exporter of bananas.

FROM CHINA TO THE WORLD

Tea is a very important drink in many parts of the world. According to legend, a Chinese emperor first drank tea more than 4,700 years ago. Early in the 17th century, Dutch trading ships carried tea from east Asia to Europe. Today, China still produces a great deal of tea. Tea plants grow well in warm, wet tropical regions, and especially in high, hilly areas. There are three main types of tea:

- green tea is made from leaves that are dried immediately after picking
- oolong tea is partially **fermented**
- black tea is allowed to ferment before being dried.

Other varieties of loose tea or teabags include names such as English breakfast, Earl Grey and souchong. Most brands label their teas according to where they come from – Chinese, Indian, Sri Lankan, Kenyan, and so on.

The world's leading tea producers, importers, and drinkers

tea produced in millions of metric tonnes (US tons)	tea imported in millions of metric tonnes (US tons)	tea consumed in kilograms (pounds) per person
India 0.9 (1.0)	Russia 0.2 (0.2)	UK 2.3 (5.1)
China 0.8 (0.9)	UK 0.2 (0.2)	Ireland 1.5 (3.3)
Sri Lanka 0.3 (0.3)	Pakistan 0.1 (0.1)	New Zealand 1.0 (2.2)
Kenya 0.3 (0.3)	USA 0.1 (0.1)	Japan 0.9 (2.0)

▼ Picking tea at a plantation in the southern Indian state of Kerala. There tea plants grow on hillsides up to 1,800 metres above sea level.

Watch the caffeine!

Children are advised not to drink tea or coffee. This is mainly because both drinks contain caffeine, which acts as a stimulant. That is why many adults do not drink coffee in the evening. They find it stops them having a good night's sleep. If they want to, they can buy decaffeinated coffee and tea.

ETHIOPIAN ORIGINS OF COFFEE

It is said that coffee was discovered in ancient Ethiopia. Goatherds noticed that their flocks would not sleep after feeding on coffee berries. As a drink, coffee reached Arabia in the 1200s and Europe 300 years later. Coffee was first grown in Brazil in the early 1700s.

Coffee plants grow well in relatively cool climates in the tropics. Today Brazil produces by far the most coffee. Many shops and restaurants label their coffee according to its origin.

▲ Coffee beans are left to dry in the sun in the Kaffa region of Ethiopia. This country, where coffee was first discovered, is still Africa's largest producer.

The world's leading coffee producers, importers, and drinkers

coffee produced in millions of metric tonnes (US tons)	coffee imported in millions of metric tonnes (US tons)	coffee consumed in kilograms (pounds) per person
Brazil 2.5 (2.8)	USA 1.2 (1.3)	Norway 10.7 (23.6)
Vietnam 0.8 (0.9)	Germany 0.9 (1.0)	Finland 10.1 (22.3)
Indonesia 0.7 (0.8)	Italy 0.4 (0.4)	Denmark 9.7 (21.4)
Colombia 0.7 (0.8)	Japan 0.4 (0.4)	Sweden 7.8 (17.2)

DAIRY PRODUCTS

Milk produced on dairy farms is turned into many other foods called dairy products. These include butter, cheese, and yoghurt. In most industrialized countries cows are raised to produce milk, and many different kinds of cheese are made from their milk. But in some parts of the world, the milk of goats, sheep, buffaloes, and even horses is used to make cheese. In northern Scandinavia, Sami herders use reindeer milk and in Tibet, people turn yaks' milk into butter and cheese.

The leading producers of milk	
Animal	**Country**
buffalo	India, Pakistan, China, Egypt, Nepal
camel	Somalia, Saudi Arabia, Sudan, Mali, United Arab Emirates
cow	USA, India, Russia, Germany, France
goat	India, Bangladesh, Sudan, Pakistan, France
sheep	China, Italy, Turkey, Greece, Syria

TRADITIONAL CHEESES

Cheese is traditionally made in different ways in various countries. The different kinds are usually named according to their origin. Buyers might not notice that their favourite cheese is not actually made in the country they expect. One of the world's most popular cheeses is Cheddar, which is a smooth, hard cheese made from cow's milk. It originated around 800 years ago in the English village of the same name.

Most of the world's Cheddar is now produced in other countries, including Australia, Canada, Ireland, New Zealand, South Africa, Sweden, and the United States. Producers are allowed to call their cheese Cheddar, which now refers more to the kind of cheese rather than the place of origin.

Some cheese names are protected. For example, Roquefort must be made from sheep's milk treated with a special mould and matured in caves near the village of Roquefort in southern France. The mould makes blue streaks in the cheese and gives it a special flavour.

Many other cheese-making villages, regions, and countries campaign to have the same protection for their names.

▲ Roquefort cheese is checked carefully.
The sheep's milk takes at least three
months to mature in special caves.

GREECE WINS FIGHT TO USE THE WORD FETA

A Yorkshire cheese producer is disappointed after a European Union
ruling stopped her using the name "feta" on her locally-produced
cheese. Judy Bell had wanted to continue calling her cheese "Yorkshire
feta", but the European Court of Justice ruled that only cheese made in
certain areas of Greece should be allowed to use the name "feta". Feta,
made from sheeps milk, has a 6,000-year history in Greece.

In the news, October 2005

Where some famous cheeses originally came from

✔ Brie: Meaux, France
✔ Edam: Edam, Netherlands
✔ Emmental: Emme Valley, Switzerland
✔ Parmesan: Parma, Italy
✔ Stilton: Stilton, UK

VEGETABLE GROUPS

Vegetables are important, **nutritious** foods that come from different parts of edible plants. We can divide them into eight different groups, from bulbs and roots under ground, to stems and leaves above it.

Wild plants were very important to prehistoric people, who hunted and gathered their food. Some of the wild varieties were planted and grown by the earliest farming communities. Experts have tried to work out where the vegetables that we eat today first grew.

Vegetables and their wild origins		
vegetable group	**examples and probable origins**	
bulb	garlic, Central Asia	leek, east Mediterranean
flower buds	broccoli, Italy	cauliflower, east Mediterranean
fruit	aubergine, India	cucumber, India
leaves	cabbage, north Europe	spinach, Iran
roots	carrot, Afghanistan	turnip, north Europe
seeds*	pea, west Asia	runner bean, Mexico
stems	asparagus, east Europe	kohlrabi, France
tubers	potato, Peru	Jerusalem artichoke, North America

* For more on seeds, see page 30.

▼ Long rows of spinach grow on this large farm in Colorado, USA.

**The world's biggest vegetable producers
in millions of metric tonnes (US tons) per year**

asparagus	aubergines	cabbages	lettuce	spinach
China 5.8 (6.4)	China 16.5 (18.2)	China 32.0 (35.3)	China 10.5 (11.6)	China 10.8 (11.9)
Peru 0.2 (0.2)	India 8.2 (9.0)	India 6.0 (6.6)	USA 4.4 (4.8)	USA 0.4 (0.4)
USA 0.1 (0.1)	Turkey 1.0 (1.1)	Russia 4.5 (5.0)	Spain 1.0 (1.1)	Japan 0.3 (0.3)
Mexico 0.07 (0.08)	Egypt 0.7 (0.8)	South Korea 2.8 (3.1)	Italy 0.9 (1.0)	Turkey 0.2 (0.2)
Germany 0.06 (0.07)	Iraq 0.4 (0.4)	USA 2.5 (2.8)	India 0.8 (0.9)	France 0.1 (0.1)

▲ Vegetables for sale at a market in southern India. Aubergines originated in India, where they are still widely grown.

China dominates the modern production of vegetables. The examples above show how much more China produces than other countries (for potatoes, see page 9). There are more than 200 million Chinese farming families, and since 1990 their food production has nearly doubled.

China has the biggest population of all the world's countries, with more than 1,300 million people – more than a fifth of the world's total. This means that most Chinese produce is needed at home. You won't find a lot of Chinese produce in your supermarket. The biggest exporters of the vegetables listed on the chart above are Peru for asparagus, Spain for aubergines and lettuce, and the United States for cabbages and spinach.

WHAT IS A NUT ... A SEED ... A PULSE?

The names of these important foodstuffs are confusing. This is mainly because they are all really seeds. A nut is actually a tree fruit with a hard outer shell around an edible kernel (sometimes called a seed). Hazelnuts and walnuts are examples of nuts. Seeds are the embryo and food supply of new plants, such as pumpkins or sunflowers. Pulses are edible seeds from a pod, such as peas, beans, and lentils, which are also classed as vegetables. Nuts, seeds, and pulses are all good sources of protein, **fibre**, vitamins, and minerals.

To which food group do peanuts belong?

We call them nuts, but peanuts are really seeds (and they belong to the family of pulses!). They are also called groundnuts because they grow under ground. The plant's flowers thrust stems into the ground, where the pods develop. Each pod usually contains two seeds. People usually call the pods shells and the seeds nuts.

MACADAMIAS

The early Aboriginal peoples of Australia were no doubt eating the nuts of the macadamia tree thousands of years ago. In the 1800s two botanists studied the tree and one of them named it after his friend, a chemist called John Macadam (1827–1865). Commercial orchards started producing nuts in the 1880s, when the tree was also introduced to Hawaii. Macadamias are also called bopple nuts, bush nuts, or Queensland nuts.

▶ Nuts are carried by a conveyor belt at a macadamia orchard in Hawaii.

Origin of some nuts and today's biggest producers

nut	origin	biggest producers
almond	south-west Asia	USA, Syria, Iran
cashew	Central America	Vietnam, India, Brazil
hazelnut	southern Europe	Turkey, Italy, USA
macadamia	Australia	Australia, USA (Hawaii), Malawi
peanut	Peru	China, India, Nigeria
pistachio	south-west Asia	Iran, USA, Turkey
walnut	west Asia	China, USA, Iran

Seedy facts

Pumpkin seeds:

✔ come from the pumpkin plant, which probably originated in North America

✔ are produced most by China, India, and Ukraine

✔ are rich in iron, zinc, and phosphorus

✔ can be eaten raw or cooked.

Sesame seeds:

✔ come from a herb that grew originally in Africa and India

✔ are used to flavour bread and biscuits

✔ are produced most by India, China, and Myanmar

✔ give a straw-coloured oil, used in cooking

✔ are ground into a paste called tahini used in humous

✔ are a good source of calcium, iron, and **niacin**.

Sunflower seeds:

✔ come from sunflowers, which belong to the daisy family and originated in North America

✔ are produced most by Russia, Ukraine, and Argentina

✔ are rich in potassium, phosphorus, iron, and calcium

✔ produce a very popular vegetable oil.

▲ Pumpkin seeds.

PACKAGING AND TRANSPORT
– how does the food get to you

The food you eat may have travelled a long way from where it was produced to where you bought it. Good packaging makes long-distance travel possible by making foods easy to handle for carriers and retailers. The packaging also protects foodstuffs from damage and protects them against dirt, harmful **bacteria**, and other dangerous substances.

Canning is a traditional method of packing food into a can to preserve it. The first canned tomatoes were produced in Pennsylvania around 1850, and canned peas followed a few years later. Californian peaches were sold in cans from the 1860s.

Raw food is prepared before canning. It is usually cleaned, peeled, cut, and sliced. It is then poured into cans automatically on a production line. The food is usually topped up with water, **brine**, sauce, or syrup, leaving a space of about 6 millimetres (0.2 inches). Some of the air in this space is removed, creating a partial **vacuum**. This makes it more difficult for bacteria to grow.

Next the can is sealed so that it is airtight. Some metal lids have a ring pull so that you don't have to use a tin-opener. Then the can is heated, killing any bacteria that might otherwise spoil the food. Finally, the can is cooled by cold water or air.

Canning facts

✔ Most food cans are made from tinplate (sheet steel coated with tin). Some are made from aluminium.

✔ Lacquers and enamels are applied to the metal, depending on intended contents.

✔ Over 32 billion food cans are used in the United States every year, and 24 billion are used in Europe.

✔ Canned food can be stored at room temperature and has a very long shelf life.

✔ Can labels give both a total weight and a drained weight. A can of chickpeas in water with a total weight of 410 grams (14.4 ounces) actually weighs 480 grams (16.9 ounces). It consists of 240 grams (8.4 ounces) of chickpeas, 170 grams (5.9 ounces) of water, and 70 grams (2.5 ounces) for the can.

▲ Picked peaches are taken away from an orchard.

QUICK COOLING

Some vegetables are cooled as soon as they are picked. They are then packed in cartons and kept cool for the trip to the market or supermarket. Vacuum cooling is much faster than ordinary cooling in a refrigerator. Picked vegetables are put into a special cooler, which allows water vapour to rise and the vegetables to cool. If they leave the field at 26°C (79°F), the vegetables can be cooled down to about 1°C (34°F) within 25 minutes.

▶ These new cans are on the production line, ready to be filled with food.

OFF TO MARKET

Since fresh foods quickly go off, they must be transported to markets and shops as rapidly as possible. Most foods are carried by road in refrigerated trucks or by rail in refrigerated wagons. For longer distances, river barges or ocean-going ships are used. Some expensive, highly **perishable** foods are flown in transport aircraft.

▼ Cartons of fish are loaded into a refrigerated truck at a port in Norway.

The distance food travels from where it is grown to where it is consumed can be calculated in so-called "food miles". As national and international trade has increased, the distances covered by food-carrying vehicles have also gone up. In the United Kingdom, for example, overall food miles increased by 50 per cent between 1980 and 2000. In the 21st century, they will increase at an even faster rate unless more efforts are made to buy local produce.

American researchers at Iowa State University found that fruit and vegetables travelled to the state's stores and supermarkets from all over the United States. This is despite the fact that Iowa has about 60,000 farms of its own. The produce that came from local farmers and suppliers travelled an average of 90 kilometres (56 miles), about a fifth of the width of the state. But the food that came from the rest of the United States travelled 2,400 kilometres (1,490 miles) on average. Out-of-state broccoli travelled more than 90 times further than in-state broccoli.

German experts studied strawberry-flavoured yoghurt on sale in Stuttgart. They found that the strawberries had been imported from Poland (which supplies 8 per cent of Germany's imported strawberries, much less than the 64 per cent from further-away Spain). The milk was from southern Germany, but the yoghurt cultures came from the north of the country. The sugar in the yoghurt was from east German beet, and the corn and wheat flour came from the Netherlands. Researchers calculated that yoghurt arriving at the production company's distribution centre had travelled an average of more than 1,000 kilometres (621 miles).

▼ Barges carry fruit and vegetables to a store in Venice, Italy, where boats are the main form of transport.

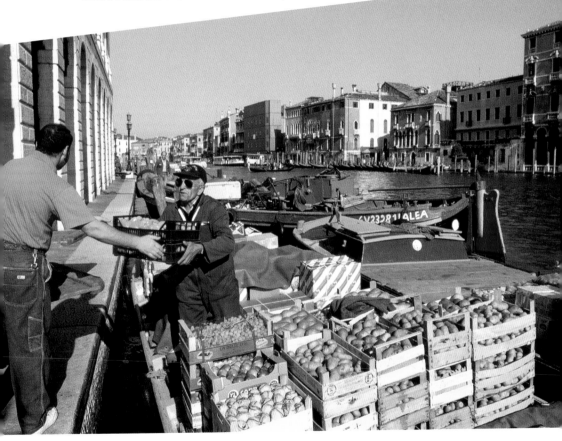

Transporting energy

Poland, United States, Italy, Ukraine, France, and the Netherlands are all in the world's top-ten producers of carrots. But European countries still import carrots from South Africa. Experts calculate that for every calorie (or energy unit) of carrot flown from South Africa to Europe, 66 calories of fuel are burned.

BUYING FOOD DIRECT

Many food producers now sell direct to their customers. Buyers place their order by phone, e-mail, or on the supplier's website, and the food is delivered to their door. The advantage of buying direct is that suppliers often tell you in their literature exactly where the food comes from, how it was produced, and how it will get to you.

Many companies sell organic food, which they advertise as "fresh from the grower". Some offer benefits that are very useful to the environment. For example, they:

- reuse cardboard or wooden delivery boxes
- use **biodegradable** plastic for box covers
- run vans on **biofuel**
- turn left-over vegetables into compost
- import some produce by ship, but never by air (because aircraft make much more pollution).

MAP PACKAGING

Producers are constantly looking for new forms of packaging. They want to protect food and prolong shelf life. One new form is called modified-atmosphere packaging (MAP). As food is wrapped in plastic, the amounts of oxygen, carbon dioxide, and other gases are changed inside the package. This "modified atmosphere" (changed air) stops bacteria growing. MAP is used for packing meat, bread, fruit, and vegetables.

A common use of MAP is for bags of lettuce. But some studies have shown that this reduces the nutritional value of the lettuce. The process removes some vitamins and **antioxidants**. So the lettuce looks very fresh and appetizing in the supermarket, but it may not be, or taste, as good as it looks. Also, the lettuce goes brown very quickly after the hi-tech pack is opened.

SALAD DAYS QUESTIONED

"Pre-packed salad leaves may not be as nutritious as they look. Research suggests a processing technique used to prolong shelf-life may remove vital nutrients. Tests showed salad bags did not boost vitamin C levels in the body like fresh lettuce. Some nutritionists say this should not deter people from eating pre-packed salad leaves as they contain other goodness such as fibre."

From BBC News at bbcnews.com © bbc.co.uk, 18 March 2003

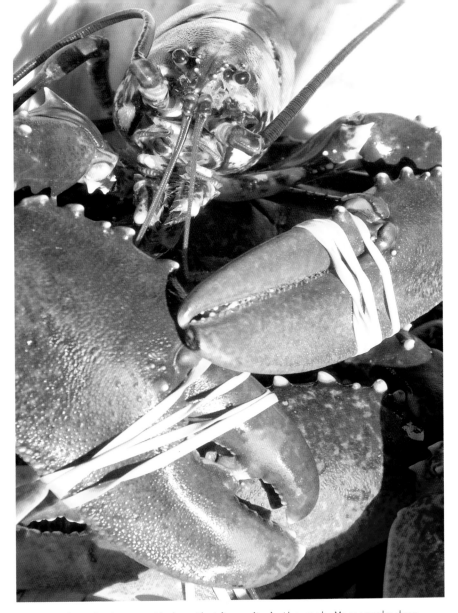

▲ This lobster's claws are tied, so that it won't nip the cook. Many cooks drop
a live lobster into a pot of boiling water to kill and then cook it. They claim the
animal feels no pain. Others consider this to be cruel.

Live lobster to your door

✔ Several companies in the US state of Maine specialize in selling live lobsters.
They catch the animals in lobster pots off the coast and store them in cooled
sea water tanks. This means they always have some available.

✔ When you order a lobster from their website, they pack it with a cold pack into
an insulated cardboard container. Then it is sent by refrigerated truck either
direct to you or to the nearest airport and then on to you. They deliver
throughout the United States by next day.

SUPERMARKETS

– where most people buy their food

Do you and your family buy most of your food in a local supermarket? That is what most people in the richer, industrialized countries of the world do. Supermarkets carry a wide range of all the major foods, and sell them at good prices. Many families do a weekly shop and get everything they need in one store.

Your grandparents may have shopped at small grocery stores for food and other household goods. They went to the greengrocer for fresh fruit and vegetables, to the butcher for meat, and to the fishmonger for fish and seafood. But times have changed for small shops, which struggle to compete with supermarkets. Only one in every six shoppers in the United Kingdom ever visits a butcher, fishmonger, or greengrocer.

▼ Shoppers check out the tinned soup and other produce in a 1950s supermarket.

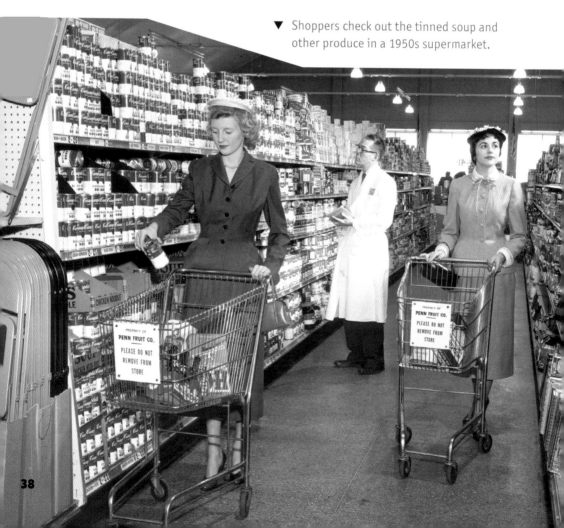

Big business

✔ In the United States, 85 per cent of perishable foods are sold in supermarkets.

✔ In the United Kingdom four large supermarket chains share three quarters of the food market. This is enormous business, and the chains employ well over half a million people.

The first supermarkets were opened in the United States in the 1930s. They sold only food and operated under the slogan, "Pile it high, sell it low". In other words, have lots of foods for shoppers to choose from and sell them at low prices. Most foods were sold loose (without packaging) and were displayed in cardboard boxes and shipping containers.

By the 1950s supermarkets had become the main outlets for food in the United States, and they soon spread through Europe. During the second half of the 20th century, they gradually added new goods to sell as well as food.

Today many supermarkets sell cooking utensils, cleaning products, greetings cards, and many other items from travel insurance to mobile telephone contracts. They even have their own banks, loyalty cards, and other financial incentives to encourage you to spend money with them.

Before the 1920s, products were fetched by a shop assistant on one side of a counter. The customers stood on the other side and asked for what they wanted. Self-service shopping helped supermarkets cut costs. Today many supermarket chains cut costs by using self-service checkout machines. Four or five machines can then be supervised by one assistant.

Most experts predict that supermarkets will continue to grow bigger and gain a larger share of the food market in future. In the future there may be no small food stores left at all. Do you think that would be a good thing?

PURCHASING POWER

Imagine you are a small farmer. If a big supermarket chain offers you a guaranteed amount of money for most of your produce for the foreseeable future, what would you do? You might be able to get a higher price for your produce locally, but that means more deliveries and less certainty of selling all your produce. **Environmentalists** say that this pressure on farmers to sell to the big supermarkets means that some supermarkets are telling farmers what to grow. If they cannot get what they want locally, the supermarkets simply buy from abroad.

SUPERMARKET PRICES

Supermarkets compete with each other to sell food at low prices. Often they try to convince shoppers that their prices are best by selling items at a very low profit or even below cost. These "loss leaders" are attractive to customers and encourage them to buy from that store.

The lowest prices are often given to "known value items" (shortened to KVIs in sales lingo), such as bread, milk, or baked beans. The idea is that people tend to know the usual price of these foods and so recognize a bargain. We base our idea of value on a few important foods. Selling food at less than cost is not allowed in some countries, to protect small shopkeepers who cannot compete.

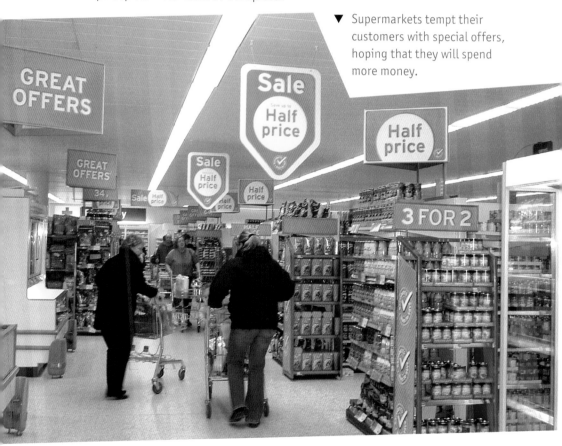

▼ Supermarkets tempt their customers with special offers, hoping that they will spend more money.

Very often you will find bread and other essential foods at the back of the supermarket. They are placed there so that you have to pass lots of other tempting items on your way. Like all products, foods sell well in shelf positions known as "hot spots". Foods positioned at eye level sell best ("eye level is buy level"), along with those in the middle of an aisle or at the end of a block of shelves.

WHERE DOES THE PACKAGING GO?

Supermarkets demand from suppliers that food items are well wrapped and packaged. This may help keep certain foods in good condition, but it is also popular with sellers because it makes food items look attractive. Do you think you might be influenced in your choice of breakfast cereal, for example, by the design of the cartons? If you're not, you are probably the exception.

The problem is that this form of marketing causes a vast amount of waste packaging. A lot of the cardboard and other material can be recycled. In some countries, such as Germany, supermarkets encourage customers to unwrap their goods after passing the checkout and leave the packaging at the store. The packaging can then be sent for recycling.

▼ Cardboard boxes are gathered at a supermarket, ready to be collected for recycling.

CONVENIENCE FOOD

– eating for ease and speed

When eating at home, many people prefer meals that can be prepared quickly and easily – convenience food. When eating out, they like their food to be delivered almost at once or within a few minutes.

The idea of fast-food restaurants started 50 years ago in the United States. Fast-food chains have since spread all around the world. The most popular serve hamburgers, pizzas, or fried chicken, and most meals come with chips.

It is important that you make careful choices at these types of restaurants. Young people should consider a children's meal, rather than a large value meal. Think about the portion-size that you need. Fast-food companies have recently started printing facts about nutritional values on menus and packaging. This is because some companies are criticized by people who claim that their food is poor quality – too fatty, too salty, or full of artificial flavours and colours. The large chains also run websites giving information about the ingredients they use and their health value.

▶ Western-style fast food in China. This busy street is in a shopping district of Shanghai.

Unfortunately these informative sites and leaflets do not usually say much about the origin of their foods. In the United States, one of the largest fast-food companies says that the beef in its burgers is "100% pure USDA inspected beef" (USDA is the United States Department of Agriculture). In the United Kingdom, the same company uses "beef bought from farms accredited by nationally recognized Farm Assurance schemes", and they state that they are a big buyer of British and Irish beef.

▶ Food bought ready to eat is popular all over the world. This woman is preparing food at a stall in a market in Vietnam.

New Zealand hoki

✔ Hoki, also known as the blue grenadier, was once thought of as an inferior species. But it has become one of the most widely used in fast-food restaurants. This has made it New Zealand's most important commercial fish species.

✔ Most of the fish caught is exported to the United States, Europe, Japan, and Australia. The total catch each year is set at a limit, so that stocks of the fish do not go down too much.

✔ In some parts of the world, fast-food restaurants use North Atlantic pollock or cod as well as hoki.

PIZZA FROM NAPLES?

No one is certain of the exact history of pizza, but it was probably first made in Naples, southern Italy. The story goes that it was a popular dish among the poor people of Naples during the 1700s. It became better known after King Umberto I visited Naples with his queen, Margherita of Savoy, in 1889. The queen enjoyed a taste of pizza and its fame soon spread.

WOW!

In 2005 a pizza company broke the world record for the furthest pizza delivery. The pizza was cooked with fresh dough in London. It travelled 16,950 kilometres (10,532 miles) and was delivered two days later in Melbourne, Australia.

Italian emigrants took recipes with them to America, where pizza also became very popular. The pizza *Margherita*, made with mozzarella cheese, tomatoes, and basil, was named after the queen. The ingredients represented the three stripes of the Italian flag – green, white, and red.

In pizza restaurants today, it's difficult to tell where all the ingredients come from. Even the pizza base is a complicated food item. One famous pizza chain lists its ingredients for pan pizza as: wheat flour, ascorbic acid, water, frozen yeast, salt, soya oil, whey powder, panadan (datem), cf05, monoglyceride, holzyme 450 (fungal alpha amylase complex), emulsifiers, monoglyceride, fatty acid esters of glycerides (calcium carbonate).

MAKING GOOD FAST FOOD CHOICES

Not all fast food is a poor choice. But it's important to balance it out by choosing a wide variety of foods. This will help you have a balanced, healthy diet. Remember to eat lots of fruit and vegetables, wholegrain versions of starchy foods when you can, and small quantities of fat, salt, and sugar.

In a fast-food restaurant you should choose:

✔ food that is grilled, **poached**, or baked, rather than fried
✔ a side salad with low fat dressing or baked potato, rather than chips
✔ mustard or ketchup, instead of mayonnaise or "special sauce"
✔ water or juice, and go easy on the cola or other fizzy drinks
✔ fruit and yoghurt, instead of sweet desserts.

Pizza varieties and Italian cities

- ✔ pizza *Fiorentina*, with spinach, Parmesan cheese, and egg: from Florence
- ✔ *Napoletana* (tomatoes, mozzarella cheese, anchovies, and capers): from Naples
- ✔ *Parmense* (asparagus, ham, and Parmesan cheese): from Parma
- ✔ *Romana* (tomatoes, mozzarella cheese, Pecorino cheese, and anchovies): from Rome
- ✔ *Siciliana* (artichoke hearts, anchovies, and ham): from Sicily
- ✔ *Veneziana* (onions, capers, olives, sultanas, and pine kernels): from Venice

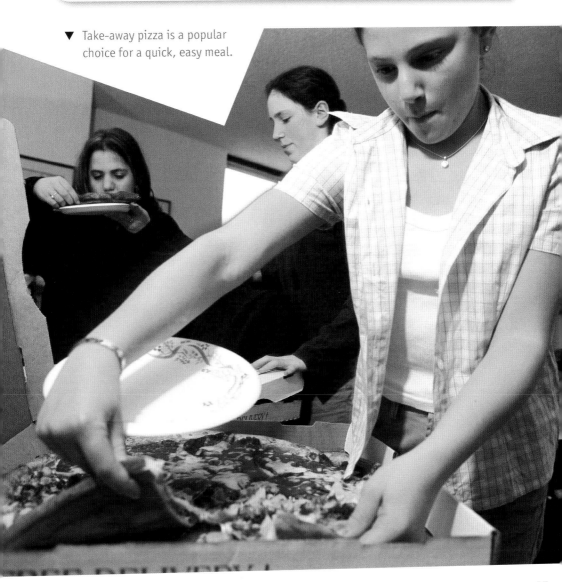

▼ Take-away pizza is a popular choice for a quick, easy meal.

LOCAL FOOD
– help limit the food miles

Would you and your family like to help keep down the food miles? If so, buy food produced locally. Local produce has become more popular in recent years, even in large cities. Shoppers buy from farmers' markets, where growers and producers from the nearby region sell their food in person direct to the public.

Registered farmers' markets in New York, London, and elsewhere in the world are checked to see that the produce is of high quality. Many sell organic produce. This is an advantage, because much of the organic food available in large supermarkets travels a long distance to the store, increasing food miles.

There are 54 farmers' markets in New York City, and 23 of them are open all year round. The others are seasonal. They are there so that 175 farmers can sell their fruit, vegetables, fish, meat, eggs, dairy, honey, maple syrup, plants, and other foods. The oldest and biggest market is at Union Square in Manhattan, New York, which first opened in 1976. It is open four days a week every week, and has become an important part of the local community. The farmers also supply produce to many local restaurants.

▶ Pumpkins for sale at Union Square farmers' market in New York.

VEGETABLES OF THE WORLD

Farmers' markets in Europe and North America sell vegetables such as beans, broccoli, cabbage, carrots, lettuce, onions, potatoes, spinach, and tomatoes. Markets in other parts of the world might sell quite different vegetables. In a small market in Kenya, Africa, many different vegetables might be on sale, such as amaranth, black nightshade, cowpeas, jute plant (or nalta jute), kale, pigweed, spider flower (or spiderwisp), and sunnhemp (or rattlebox). Many of these plants also grow elsewhere, but are rarely used as food in other parts of the world.

▼ Beans, seeds, and pulses form just part of the produce in this colourful market in Kenya.

Micro-livestock

Would you fancy eating insects? If so, you might like the markets in the following countries, where edible insects are sold. Some are very nutritious. Gram for gram, termites have twice as much protein as beef. But don't ever eat any insects at home – they might be poisonous!

✔ Mexico – grasshoppers (for frying), agave worms

✔ Colombia – termites, palm grubs, ants (used as a spread on toast)

✔ Philippines – June beetles, mole crickets, dragonfly larvae

✔ Papua New Guinea – sago grubs (for boiling or roasting), stick insects

47

IDEAS FOR HEALTHY EATING

People eat nutritious food all over the world. This does more than keep people healthy – it adds pleasure to their lives. Here are some favourite healthy dishes from the world's six continents.

AUSTRALASIA

- Beef is popular in Australia, along with lamb, pork, and poultry. Meat is often grilled on a barbecue and served with potatoes and vegetables.
- In New Zealand, lamb is a favourite, served with *kumara* (sweet potatoes); and soup made with *toheroa*, a native green clam.
- Pacific islanders have lived for centuries on seafood; they cook crabs, lobsters, shrimps, as well as fish, along with a root vegetable called *taro*.

EUROPE

Dishes from France and Italy are popular all over the world, for example:

- French *ratatouille* – onions, tomatoes, peppers, courgettes, and aubergines, stewed in olive oil
- Italian *spaghetti alle vongole* – strings of pasta with clams.

ASIA

In China, rice is generally served with every meal, such as:

- stir-fried crispy seaweed and spring rolls
- pork *chow mein*, thinly sliced pork fillets with peppers, spring onions, bean sprouts, and noodles stir-fried with sesame oil
- chicken and noodle soup with bamboo shoots, grated ginger, and mushrooms.

In India, foods are highly seasoned with spices:

- *biriani pilau*, flavoured rice with turmeric, coriander, green chilli, and cumin, cooked with boned lamb, chicken, or fish
- *parathas*, Indian bread stuffed with spiced potato purée and minced onion or minced meat and lentils
- *aloo saag*, spinach, potatoes, and Indian spices.

Why "hamburger"?

German immigrants took steak from Hamburg to America in the 19th century. The first "hamburgers" (Hamburg steak in a bun) were sold at the St Louis World Fair in 1904.

AFRICA

- A favourite dish in northern Africa is couscous (see page 21). A stew of meat, fish, and vegetables is cooked in the lower part of a stock-pot, and the couscous is steamed in the upper part.
- Meat and fish stews are also cooked in a *tagine*. This is a shallow dish with a conical lid, ideal for long, slow simmering.
- Moroccan *briouats* and Algerian *boureks* are triangular dough parcels filled with chicken and spinach.
- In South Africa, *potjie kos* is very popular. A *potjie* is a heavy three-legged pot that is used on an open fire. Any type of meat and mixture of vegetables is slowly stewed in it.

NORTH AMERICA

Some well-known specialities:

- New England clam chowder, a soup with clams, potatoes, and onions cooked in milk and cream
- Boston baked beans, dried soya beans with salt pork, dark brown sugar, and mustard baked in a casserole for 4–5 hours
- Mexican tortillas, flat thin maize pancakes with fillings, such as shredded chicken breast, chillies, and tomatoes.

SOUTH AMERICA

Some favourite dishes:

- Brazilian *feijoada*, a meat stew with black beans and rice.
- Colombian *ajiaco* soup, with potatoes, chicken, corn, and cassava.

▲ Muslim men eating a meal together in Morocco, North Africa.

RECIPES

DHAL

As an ingredient in Indian food, dhal is split pulses. They can be split chickpeas, lentils, or beans. Dhal is eaten with bread, rice, and curried vegetables. This recipe, which comes from Bengal, uses red lentils, which are very high in vitamin B 6. The golden turmeric powder comes from the ground root of a south Asian plant.

Ingredients:
250 g (9 ounces) red lentils
3 cups water
3 tablespoons vegetable oil
2 small onions, finely chopped
2 garlic cloves, finely chopped
$\frac{1}{2}$ fresh green chilli, seeded
    and finely chopped
$\frac{1}{2}$ teaspoon ground turmeric
2 dried red chillies, crushed
1 teaspoon ground coriander
$\frac{1}{2}$ teaspoon ground cumin
$\frac{1}{2}$–1 teaspoon salt
3 teaspoons lemon juice
3 tablespoons fresh coriander,
    chopped

▲ Ingredients for a delicious dhal dish.

Method:
Wash the lentils and put them in a medium-sized pan. Add the water and bring to the boil. Add the turmeric, cover and simmer for 15–20 minutes, or until the lentils are very soft. Mash the lentils with a fork and mix in the salt. Heat the oil in a small frying pan and gently cook the onion, without browning, for about 8 minutes. Add the garlic and green chilli and cook for another 3 minutes. Combine the ground coriander, cumin, crushed red chilli, and lemon juice in a small bowl. Add one teaspoon of water and mix to a paste. Stir the paste into the onion mixture and fry for 2–3 minutes. Pour over the reserved lentils in the pan and mix well. Return to the heat, cover and simmer for 10 minutes. Stir once or twice to make sure the mixture does not stick to the bottom. The dhal should be like porridge. If it's too dry, add a little more water. Sprinkle with chopped coriander and serve hot. Serves 4–6 people.

▲ This fruit salad will give you
a real vitamin boost.

EXOTIC FRUIT SALAD

You can use whichever fruits are in season and available in your local
market. Guavas have lots of vitamin C.

Ingredients:

1 large mango

1 papaya

1 guava

1 pineapple

2 bananas

1/2 melon

2 passion fruits (granadillas)

juice and grated rind of 1 lime

juice of 1 orange

1 tablespoon sesame seeds

2 kiwi fruits, peeled and sliced

Method:

Peel and cut the mango, papaya, guava, pineapple, bananas, and melon
into small pieces and put into a large bowl. Cut the passion fruits in half
and scoop out the seeds with a teaspoon. Add them to the bowl. Mix in
the juice and rind of the lime, and the orange juice. Sprinkle with sesame
seeds and decorate with kiwi slices. Serve with Greek yoghurt. Serves
4–6 people.

GLOSSARY

agents people who organize things, such as buying and selling, for others

antioxidants substances that stop certain chemical reactions causing food to decay

bacteria (plural of bacterium) single-celled microscopic organisms

battery hens female chickens kept in batteries (series of cages) for their eggs

biodegradable made of a substance that can be broken down by bacteria or in other natural ways. It therefore does not cause pollution.

biofuel fuel produced from plant or animal matter, such as sugar cane or vegetable oil

brine salt water

cereal grains seeds from cereal plants such as maize, wheat, or rice

corporation large company or group of companies

crop plants grown for food

cured (of food) made to last longer by smoking, drying, or salting

deplete reduce or use up

embryo part of a seed that grows into a new plant

endangered in danger of dying out

environmentalists people who care about and act to protect nature

export sell goods to another country and send them there. The goods are called exports.

factory ship large fishing vessel that can freeze its own catch on board

fermented broken down by a substance such as yeast or bacteria

fertilizer chemical or natural substance added to soil to provide plants with nutrients to help them grow

fibre substances in plants that help people digest the food they have eaten

husk outer covering of some grains and nuts

import buy goods from another country. The goods are called imports.

intensive farming using technology to produce as much food as possible

kernel grain of a cereal plant that contains a seed and husk

leguminous belonging to a family of plants that have seeds in pods, such as peas

manure animal dung used as fertilizer

mineral solid chemical substance that occurs naturally in the soil. We need certain minerals in small quantities to be healthy.

niacin type of vitamin B

nitrogen gas that makes up a large part of air

nutrient substance in food that provides nourishment (helping us grow and be healthy)

nutritious helping growth and health

omega-3 type of unsaturated fatty acid mainly found in oily fish and in other foods such as milk

perishable likely to decay and go bad quickly

pesticides chemical substances used to destroy pests, especially insects

poached cooked by simmering in or over boiling water

protein natural substance made up of amino acids that acts as a nutrient in food

sorghum cereal plant grown for its grain

surplus more of something than needed

vacuum space from which all air has been removed

vitamin one of a group of substances we need to be healthy

world trade network system that links traders across the world, allowing them to buy from and sell to each other

FINDING OUT MORE

GROWING YOUR OWN FOOD

Growing your own food is the most local food you can get, with zero food miles! If you have a garden or backyard, or even some pots or tubs, you could try your hand at growing herbs or vegetables. There may also be allotments near you, where you can share a plot. You will find lots of books on the subject in your local library or bookshop. You might also find tips and further ideas at a garden centre, where you can buy seeds.

VISIT A FARM

A real working farm will give you an idea of how food is produced on a small scale. But do not just turn up at a farm and hope for a good reception. Look for a list of working farms on the Internet, from your local council, tourism board, or information centre, and contact them to arrange a visit.

LOOK CLOSELY AT LABELS

If you live in or near a big town or city, look for stores, mini-markets, or delicatessens that sell food from different cultures. Look closely at the labels to see where the food comes from. You might like to try a different version of a food that you like.

BOOKS

Body Needs: titles include *Carbohydrates for a healthy body*, *Proteins for a healthy body*, and *Fats for a healthy body,* (Heinemann Library, 2003). This series looks at what the human body needs to function healthily.

Chain Reactions: From DNA to GM Wheat, Sally Morgan (Heinemann Library, 2006). Learn more about genetically modified foods.

Eyewitness Guide: Food, Laura Buller (Dorling Kindersley, 2005)

Penguin Companion to Food, Alan Davidson (Penguin, 2002)

Planet Under Pressure: Food, Paul Mason (Raintree, 2005)

Trends in Food Technology: titles include *Food and Consumers, The Food Industry,* and *Food Ingredients,* (Heinemann Library, 2005)

A World of Recipes: titles include *Indonesia, Egypt, Spain, Russia, Vietnam,* and *Vegetarian recipes from around the World,* (Heinemann Library, 2002)

WEBSITES

www.defra.gov.uk
UK Department for Environment, Food and Rural Affairs (Defra) aims to "work for the essentials of life – food, air, land, water, people, animals, and plants".

www.food.gov.uk
The main website of the Food Standards Agency (FSA), an independent UK government department.

www.eatwell.gov.uk
An FSA website that provides consumer advice and information on healthy eating.

www.affa.gov.au
The website of the Australian Department of Agriculture, Fisheries, and Forestry.

www.fairtrade.net
For more information on Fairtrade visit the international website. Fairtrade also has websites in countries such as:
- Australia – **www.fta.org.au**
- UK – **www.fairtrade.org.uk**

www.fao.org
Visit the Food and Agricultural Organization of the United Nations for food statistics from around the world.

www.nutrition.org.uk
The British Nutrition Foundation is a charitable organization that raises funds from the food industry, UK government, and other sources. It aims to promote the nutritional well-being of society.

www.foodtech.org.uk
A site for students and teachers on food technology.

www.foodstandards.gov.au
Food labels differ around the world; this site contains useful information about food labels from Australia and New Zealand.

INDEX

Making Healthy Food Choices titles include:

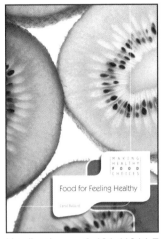

Hardback   0 431 11914 7

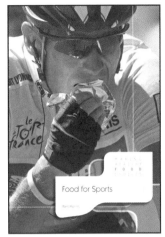

Hardback   0 431 11915 5

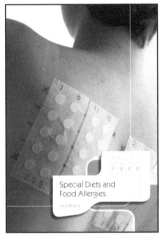

Hardback   0 431 11916 3

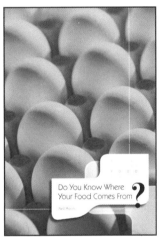

Hardback   0 431 11917 1

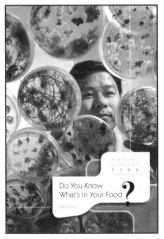

Hardback   0 431 11918 X

Find out about other titles from Heinemann Library on our website www.heinemann.co.uk/library